Written by Clive Gifford
Illustrations by Emiliano Migliardo

Cover typography based on designs by Thy Bui.

First published in Great Britain in 2023 by Red Shed, part of Farshore

An imprint of HarperCollins*Publishers*
1 London Bridge Street, London SE1 9GF
www.farshore.co.uk

HarperCollins*Publishers*
Macken House, 39/40 Mayor Street Upper
Dublin 1, D01 C9W8

Copyright © HarperCollins*Publishers* Limited 2023

ISBN 978 0 00 861578 9

Printed and bound in the UK using 100% renewable
electricity at CPI Group (UK) Ltd

001

A CIP catalogue record for this title is available from the British Library.

Stay safe online. Any website addresses listed in this book are correct at the time of going
to print. However, Farshore is not responsible for content hosted by third parties. Please be
aware that online content can be subject to change and websites can contain content that is
unsuitable for children. We advise that all children are supervised when using the internet.

AMAZING
FOOTBALL
FACTS
FOR EVERY 8 YEAR OLD

RED
SHED

If you love watching or playing football, you'll find **TONS** of fascinating facts in this fun-filled book ...

Which animal correctly guessed the outcome of every 2010 World Cup match that Germany played?

Where was the world's oldest surviving football found?

Which club's crest features Santa Claus?

Read on to find out the answers and lots more awesome information about the beautiful game ...

San Marino's national football club have only won one match since their first official game in 1990.

Their only victory so far was when they beat Liechtenstein 1–0 in 2004. The team has let in over 780 goals and scored less than 35!

There is a football World Cup for robots!

The RoboCup kicked off in Nagoya, Japan, in 1997. There were 39 teams in total and two winners in different leagues: the small robot league and the medium-sized robot league.

Former US President Barack Obama played a brief game of football with a robot.

His opponent was ASIMO, a 1.3m-tall
humanoid robot that could run, as well
as kick and control a football.

Two Harvard students developed a football that can generate electricity.

Julia Silverman and Jessica Matthews invented the Soccket, which turns the energy created when the ball is kicked into electricity stored in a battery inside the ball.

Playing for 30 minutes can provide up to three hours worth of power!

**In the Morro de Mineira favela –
a deprived area of the Brazilian capital,
Rio de Janeiro – the world's first
electricity-generating football pitch
was installed in 2014.**

The pitch has 200 tiles underneath artificial turf, which turn the movement of players stepping on them into electricity. In turn, this powers the pitch's six LED floodlights.

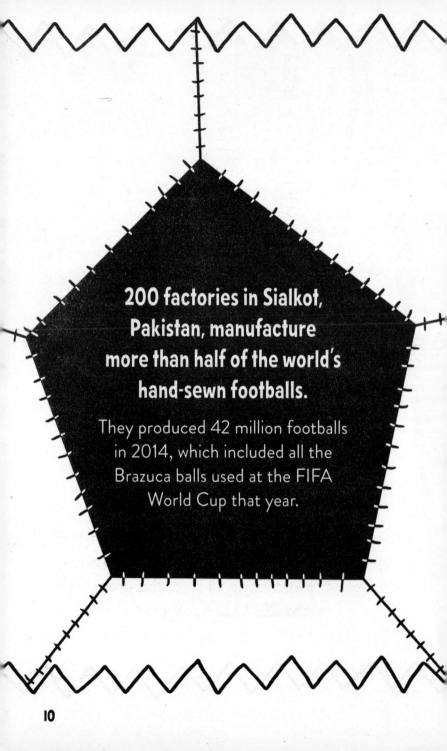

200 factories in Sialkot, Pakistan, manufacture more than half of the world's hand-sewn footballs.

They produced 42 million footballs in 2014, which included all the Brazuca balls used at the FIFA World Cup that year.

Footballs used in World Cup tournaments are tested using a robot leg.

Modern designs are kicked at least 2,000 times by a robot leg, and the Brazuca ball was tested by 600 professional footballers for the 2014 tournament.

There is such thing as horse football!

Yes, really! The game uses most of football's regular rules, except that it is played on horseback, with a giant inflatable ball. The Equine Soccer League was formed in the US in 2009 to coordinate this growing sport.

An unusual, unofficial World Cup competition featuring elephants as players took place in Thailand in 2014.

The elephants could thump the ball with their feet, although some 'cheated' and carried the ball with their trunks!

In the 1600s, the Powhatan Native American peoples played a football-like game called Pasuckuakohowog.

The name literally means 'they gather to play ball with the foot'. It was played on a humungous pitch with goals that were 800m wide, and games could last all day. It's thought that each team could contain hundreds of players!

For centuries, indigenous Inuit peoples in Canada played a version of football on snow and ice called Aqsaqtuk.

It was played with a ball made of animal hide, stuffed with moss, moose hair and feathers. The goal area could be up to 16km wide!

The Maya, an ancient indigenous civilisation that lived in modern-day Central America, played a kicking ball game called Ti Pitziil.

The ancient city of Tikal has five narrow ball courts with sloping stone walls, where the Maya would play with a solid rubber ball. Although the game was usually played for fun, it would sometimes be used to settle arguments, and the losing team would be punished with torture, or even execution!

In Japan, before there was football, there was Kemari.

Originally from China, the game involved players wearing traditional dress and keeping a ball made from deerskin in the air using any part of their body, except their hands and arms. One of the first documented games in Japan took place in 644CE.

Calcio Fiorentino is a type of football game that originated in Florence, Italy, over 500 years ago.

The game has 27 players per side, and everyone uses their hands and feet to control the ball. It used to be played by nobles, including at least three popes, and in the winter, it would even be played on the iced-over Arno river that runs through the city. It's still played today!

In preparation for the 2014 World Cup in Brazil, Germany built an entire training base called Campo Bahia.

It had 14 villas, 65 rooms, a swimming pool, spa and full-sized football pitch. The German team shipped out over 20 tonnes of kit, including mountain bikes and table-tennis tables.

It must have helped, as the Germans won the tournament that year!

Three-sided football is played by three teams with three goals and one ball.

With a special pitch and opponents' goals either side of their own, players need to know their angles. A three-sided football league began in Australia in 2014.

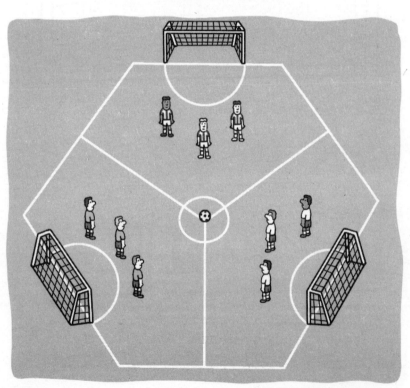

Footdoubleball was devised in Ukraine in 2007.

The game is played with two different coloured footballs that are in play at the same time. It was created by students at a university in the country's capital, Kyiv.

Three ships moored near the North Pole staged a football tournament in 2001.

The matches were played on ice and featured teams from the crews of the *Oden* from Sweden, the *Healy* from the USA and Germany's *Polarstern*.

The Germans won.

In the same year, a football game was played on the snow-covered top of South America's second-highest mountain.

Two teams – one made up of international guides and mountaineers, the other of local people from Bolivia – climbed the peak and played two 20-minute halves using orange-coloured footballs.

The first recorded women's football match took place on 9th May 1881.

It was played in Edinburgh between teams from Scotland and England. Victorian dress was very strict at the time, and players had to wear corsets, heeled boots and bonnets – very difficult for heading the ball!

Lily Parr was the first British female player to feature in the National Football Museum Hall of Fame.

She was also the first female football player in the UK to be honoured with a statue.

Gustavo Llanos is a Colombia supporter who dresses as the country's national bird at every national team game!

He dresses up as a bright orange, blue and red giant condor bird, and other fans would sometimes suspend him from ropes so that he could hang down from the stadium.

In the 1970s, Alfred Baloyi invented the Makarapa, a hat that is now worn by football fans in South Africa.

He took a miner's hard hat and decorated it with things like football badges, signs and horns. It is often worn with giant glasses, and one football fan, Sadaam Maake, has a collection of over 200 different designs!

A Brazilian shopkeeper named his son after multiple players from France's 2006 World Cup team.

After enjoying two years living in France, Petrucio Santos named his son Zinedine Yazid Zidane Thierry Henry Barthez Eric Felipe Silva Santos!

A Norwegian couple, who are avid Liverpool fans, named their daughter after the club's anthem.

Their daughter is called Karoline YNWA – her middle name being an abbreviation of the beloved Liverpool Football Club song 'You'll Never Walk Alone'.

From 1980 up until his death in 2022, Kenya superfan Isaac Juma Onyango did not miss a single home match.

He was given a lifetime achievement award by Kenya's football association in 2010.

Three fans of Russian football club Zenit Saint Petersburg drove 8,000km across the country to see one of the team's games in 2006.

Their car broke down at their destination, where Zenit Saint Petersburg were playing against fellow Russian team Luch-Energiya, and they had to take a long, slow train all the way back home. However, the team repaid their fans' loyalty by giving them a brand-new car!

In honour of the United Arab Emirates' most famous football fan, restaurant owner Khaled Al-Hammadi, a street was named after him.

Khaled had faithfully followed the national team everywhere since 1974, and always carried a large megaphone to cheer them on!

In Italy, just one supporter turned up to watch Udinese Calcio in their 2012 Serie A away game against Sampdoria.

Loyal fan Arrigo Brovedani was first booed by the home fans before later being cheered on, given a football shirt by Sampdoria and invited out for a meal. Brovedani's favourite team won 2–0!

The Church of Maradona was set up in 1998 by fans of legendary Argentine footballer Diego Maradona.

The 'church' followers celebrate Christmas on Maradona's birthday (30th October) and adopt Diego as their middle name!

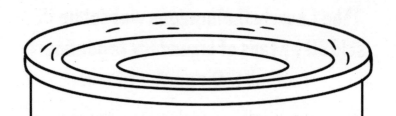

In 1999, Italian Serie A football club Fiorentina sold tin cans containing air collected from their Artemio Franchi stadium.

The unusual items of football merchandise were sold in three versions: 'Air of the Terraces', 'Dressing Room Atmosphere' and 'Essence of Victory'.

The San Jose Earthquakes club in the US sold clay heads of striker Steven Lenhart as merchandise!

The clay heads held soil so that fans could plant chia seeds, which grow quickly to form the player's long hair.

The longest international football career lasted 27 years and 319 days.

Despite being retired, Giorgios (Yórghos) Koúdas was invited to play in one final game for Greece against Yugoslavia in 1995. His first game for Greece had been against Australia in 1967!

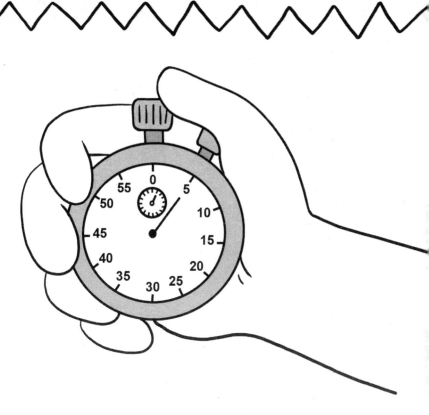

The shortest international football career lasted only five seconds!

Defender Franck Jurietti proudly made his debut for the French national team at the Stade de France in 2005 against Cyprus. He came on with only five seconds of the game to play and never played for his country again.

A small black dog interrupted the 1962 World Cup quarter-final between England and Brazil!

The dog started chasing the ball before being caught by England striker Jimmy Greaves. A member of the Brazilian team, winger Garrincha, later adopted the dog and called it Bi.

During a 2016 match between two of Ecuador's top league teams, a swarm of bees flew on to the pitch.

The bees terrorised the players so much that the referee had to stop the game. It was re-played two days later.

TOING

A goal was scored during the 2009 English Premier League using a red beach ball!

A Liverpool fan threw the ball on to the pitch, and Sunderland striker Darren Bent made a shot that bounced off the beach ball and into the net. The goal was allowed and Sunderland won the match 1–0!

A ball boy cheekily scored a goal in a 2006 match between Brazilian clubs Santacruzense and Atletico Sorocaba.

After the home team (Santacruzense) shot the football wide, the boy tapped the ball into the net when the referee had his back turned. The goal was awarded!

The Chilean football team consumed the traditional food and drinks of their opponents before their 1962 World Cup matches.

They ate cheese before defeating Switzerland, gobbled spaghetti before beating Italy, and drank vodka before beating the Soviet Union 2–1 and reaching the semi-final!

Beans on toast may be the key to success.

The Lionesses' Georgia Stanway always likes
to eat a pre-match meal of beans on toast.
As superstitions go, it's a tasty one!

Former Veracruz defender Oscar Mascorro took pre-match rituals to a whole new level.

He would always get out of bed on his right foot
first; have a hamburger, apple juice, and vanilla
milkshake as his pre-match meal; write 'M' and
'P' in honour of his parents on bandages on his
wrists and pull out a piece of the turf when he
walked onto the pitch!

When Jamaica qualified for the 1998 World Cup, a giant inflatable ball was constructed and displayed in the country!

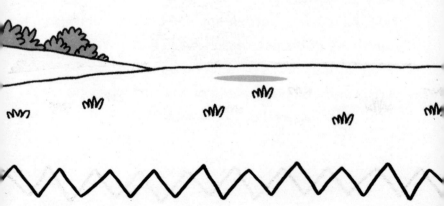

It was approximately 15.5m in diameter, with its panels containing good luck messages from fans. The ball was also displayed in New York, London and, finally, Paris, where the World Cup was being held that year.

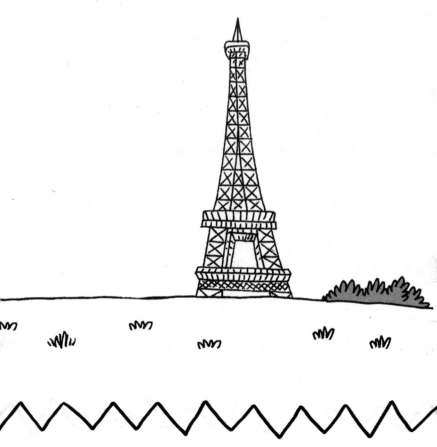

There is a football club called FC Santa Claus!

The home ground of this Finnish club resides in a city on the edge of the Arctic Circle. As well as playing in red and white, their club crest features Santa Claus.

The club badge of Czech team Bohemians 1905 features a kangaroo.

As they were about to sail home from a tour of Australia in 1927, the team was presented with two kangaroos, which were given to Prague Zoo when they reached home.

Guus Hiddink, South Korea's coach at the 2002 World Cup, was generously rewarded for getting the team to the semi-finals.

South Korea was the first team from Asia ever to reach a World Cup semi-final, and Hiddink was given a free villa on Jeju Island, South Korea, as well as free flights for life with Korean Air.

Saudi Arabian footballer Saeed Al-Owairan was awarded a Rolls Royce car after his exceptional performance at the 1994 World Cup.

In a match against Belgium, he ran 70m with the ball to score what is considered one of the best goals in World Cup history. He was later named Asian Footballer of the Year.

An Argentinian club considered implanting microchips with fans' season ticket details into their bodies.

The idea behind Club Atlético Tigre's proposal in 2016 was that the fans would never have to worry about leaving their tickets at home!

What is thought to be the world's most expensive football ticket was bought for £2.2 million!

A businessperson from Saudi Arabia paid the huge sum for a VIP ticket in a charity bid to watch Cristiano Ronaldo and Lionel Messi face each other in January 2023.

The bids started at £220,000.

Referees' whistles were first used in football in 1878.

English inventor Joseph Hudson began manufacturing whistles that were first used by police forces in the 1870s.

FFRRRRP!

By 2000, his company, J Hudson & Co, had sold over 200 million Acme Thunderer whistles, many used to stop and start football matches all over the world!

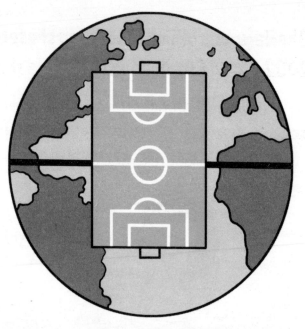

The Estádio Milton Corrêa is perched right on the Equator (the imaginary line that runs around the middle of the Earth's surface).

The football pitch's halfway line runs along the Equator, meaning that one half of the pitch is in the northern half of the planet and the other is in the southern half.

The Jeju World Cup Stadium, built for the 2002 World Cup in South Korea, is shaped like the mouth of a volcano.

It was built 14m below the ground to avoid high winds, and its roof resembles the fishing nets traditionally used in the region.

The Estádio Municipal in Portugal is in an old quarry.

One end of the stadium is a solid rock face that doesn't have any seats. To move from one side of the stadium to the other, fans have to walk through an underground tunnel.

Islanders on Koy Panyi, a floating village in Thailand, built a football pitch on the sea!

As the islanders live in houses built on stilts, there was not enough land for a football pitch. The floating football pitch doesn't have any nets or barriers surrounding it, so if the ball is kicked out, players have to dive into the water to get it!

The home ground of a Slovakian team has a railway track running through it.

The track runs between the pitch and the supporters' stand, and steam trains run even during matches. Sometimes the games are obscured by all the smoke. Choo choo!

Croatian football stadium Batarija has a UNESCO World Heritage site at each goal.

The stadium is the home ground of the HNK Trogir team. It has the tower of St Marco at one end and the 15th-century Kamerlengo Castle at the other. What a view!

The first Women's World Cup was held in 1991 in China.

This was a whopping 61 years after the first men's World Cup, played in 1930. The United States team was the first to lift the women's trophy.

The 1999 Women's World Cup final set a world record for the number of people watching a women's sports event.

A huge 90,185 people watched the US go head-to-head with China at the Rose Bowl stadium in California, USA. It was 0–0 at full time, but the Americans triumphed 5–4 in the penalty shootouts.

The 2015 Women's World Cup, held in Canada, was the first ever to be played on artificial turf.

Artificial grass was developed in the 1960s.

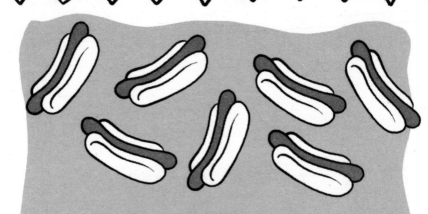

The 2010 World Cup was the first to be held on the African continent.

It was a rousing success, and a total of 3,178,856 people attended the 64 matches, eating 390,600 hot dogs and drinking more than 750,000 litres of beer!

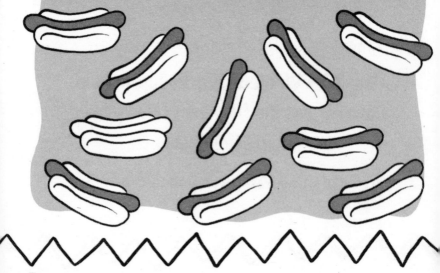

An octopus correctly predicted the outcome of all seven of Germany's matches during the 2010 World Cup.

Paul the octopus headed towards one of two plastic boxes containing food and bearing the national flags of whichever two teams were playing a game, correctly predicting all of Germany's wins and defeats.

The first game in Italy where footballers could be shown a green card took place in 2016.

The card was used to praise players for friendly or fair behaviour, and was first seen in a match between second division Italian teams Spezia Calcio and Bari. The player with the most green cards at the end of the 2016–7 season received an award.

Former Colombian footballer Gerardo Bedoya received more red cards than any other footballer in history.

Nicknamed 'The Beast', he was shown 46 red cards throughout his playing career. During his first match as an assistant coach, he was sent to the stands after insulting the referee for ten minutes.

FootGolf is a hybrid of football and golf that began in the Netherlands in 2008.

Players have to kick a regular-sized football off the tee and try to get the ball into an oversized golf hole in as few kicks as possible.

Foot Darts was created in 2016.

Players kick Velcro-covered footballs at a 7m-tall inflatable dartboard. Players score points by kicking the ball into the scoring zones.

The first public football match on roller skates took place at the Alexandra Skating Rink in Derby, UK, in 1883.

This five-a-side game is now a fully-fledged sport, and the first Rollersoccer World Cup was held in London 120 years after the first public match.

The first Beach Soccer World Championships started in Rio de Janeiro, Brazil, in 1995.

Beach soccer is a five-a-side game with footballers playing in bare feet. The tournament kicked off on Copacabana Beach, and host country Brazil were the first winners.

In the same year, the first World Blind Soccer Championships were held in Argentina.

Visually impaired players use a special ball with bells inside so they can hear it as it travels around the pitch.

Autoball was first played on the pitch in 1933.

The game involves two cars per side nudging a giant football around the pitch. Vroom!

Italian footballer Giuseppe Meazza's shorts fell down during a match!

He was about to take a penalty during the 1938 World Cup semi-final. Luckily, he was able to hold up his shorts with one hand and scored the winning goal. Oops!

Goalkeeper Willie Fotheringham, who played for Scottish team Queen of the South, once left his false teeth in the back of his goal and forgot to pick them up!

The year was 1935, and Willie's teeth were returned to him on a fish delivery truck the following week!

As well as being a former professional footballer ...

... Australia's John Kundereri is also an artist.

He was selected for the Australian national football squad in 1960. He founded an art studio when he retired, and one of his best-known works involved painting two airplanes in traditional indigenous patterns.

Three-time Russian Premier League winner Andrey Arshavin is a fashion designer!

He studied fashion at the St Petersburg State University of Technology and Design and has designed ranges of women's clothing. Several of his fashion creations are on display at the university's museum.

Maria Mutola from Mozambique became a footballer after retiring from her career in athletics.

As well as winning ten World Championship athletic titles and an Olympic gold medal in the 800m in 2000, she played her first match for the Mozambique women's national football team in 2011. The team won 1–0 against Swaziland.

Former Croatia captain, now manager, Slaven Bilić is also a rock guitarist!

He began and ended his career as a professional footballer with the HNK Hajduk Split team, but he played with the band Rawbau in his spare time. Their single 'Vatreno Ludilo' ('Fiery Madness') was recorded for Croatia's performance at the 2008 EUROs.

Former professional footballer Hannes Thór Halldórsson from Iceland is also a filmmaker.

A year after he joined Iceland's national team in 2011, he directed Iceland's Eurovision Song Contest entry video. He has also directed adverts and short movies.

Lioness Jill Scott was a talented long-distance runner before turning to football.

She ran with Sunderland Harriers, winning the North of England Under-13 cross-country title and the Junior Great North Run.

President George Weah of Liberia used to be a professional footballer.

Before becoming a senator and being elected as president in 2018, George Weah played for clubs in Liberia, Monaco, England, Italy, France, UAE, Cameroon and Ivory Coast. He was the first African footballer to be awarded FIFA World Player of the Year in 1995, and he used some of his earnings to fund the Liberian national team.

The average speed of a Mexican wave at a football stadium is about 22 seats per second.

A Mexican wave is when the crowd stands with their arms raised, then sits in turn to create the impression of a wave running around the stands.

Fans of several different football teams perform an unusual crowd move called the Poznań.

Originally called the 'Grecque' in the 1960s, it involves the crowd turning their backs to the pitch, putting their arms around each other and jumping up and down while chanting. It was first performed by fans of Polish team Lech Poznań.

The world's oldest professional footballer is 56-year-old Kazuyoshi Miura from Japan.

Nicknamed 'King Kazu', he made his debut in 1986 and currently plays for Yokohama Football Club. He played for Japan on 89 occasions between 1990 and 2000, scoring 55 goals, and is the country's second-highest goal scorer.

Brazilian midfielder Formiga is the oldest footballer to compete in the FIFA Women's World Cup.

She was 41 years and 112 days old when she played in Brazil's quarter-final match against France in 2019. Formiga is also the only player, male or female, to have played in seven FIFA World Cups.

The record for the most people playing keepy-uppy (keeping a football in the air) in one place is 1,406.

About one fifth of the population of Caerano di San Marco, a small town in Italy, took part in this record-breaking feat in 2016.

In 2016, Abraham Muñoz ran an entire marathon while keeping a football in the air with his feet and head.

It took him 5 hours and 41 minutes to complete the distance and he only dropped the ball four times!

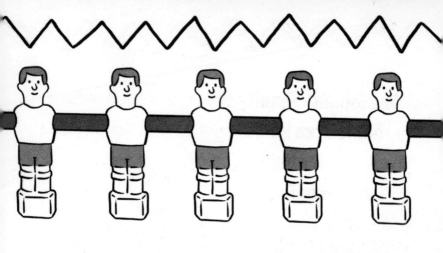

The longest table football game lasted 61 hours and 17 minutes – more than five days!

Four men from Austria played a marathon game of doubles in 2012, and over 6,000 goals were scored.

The longest penalty shootout ended with a record-breaking 54 penalty kicks taken.

English clubs Washington and Bedlington drew 3–3 at full time during a 2022 match and relentlessly challenged each other as they scored goal after goal during penalties. The game ended 25–24 to Washington, and out of the 54 penalties taken by both teams, 49 were scored.

The chairman of a Turkish football club banned beards in 2014.

Determined to portray the club's players as model sportsmen, Ilhan Cavcav told players he would fine them 25,000 Turkish lira (around £7,000) if any of them grew a beard.

Former Manchester City manager Roberto Mancini banned his players from wearing the colour purple.

After the team's poor performance during the 2012–3 Premier League season, Mancini believed the colour was unlucky and had their partly purple club tracksuits replaced with a purple-free design. At one game, he refused to let players wear purple UEFA warm-up bibs!

The king of Romania selected the country's squad for the first ever World Cup in 1930.

Instead of the coach, King Carol II chose the members of the squad, travelled with the team to Uruguay on the SS Conte Verde and took part in football training with them on deck.

By 1970, Brazil had won the World Cup three times, and they were allowed to keep the Jules Rimet Trophy forever.

However, the trophy was stolen from the headquarters of the Brazilian Football Confederation in Rio de Janeiro in 1983 and has never been recovered.

A 14-year-old boy decided whether Spain or Turkey would appear at the 1954 World Cup.

As the two countries tied during their World Cup qualifier match, teenager Luigi Franco Gemma was blindfolded and picked lots to send Turkey through to the tournament.

To celebrate the 2010 World Cup in South Africa, the world's biggest working vuvuzela horn was built.

The vuvuzela horn is blown at many matches in South Africa, and a giant version that was 35m long and 5.5m in diameter at its widest point was built. It was so large that it had to be blown by air compressors!

The world's most expensive football is valued at around £2 million.

Cape Town jeweller Yair Shimansky celebrated the 2010 World Cup held in South Africa by creating a football that was covered in 6,620 white diamonds and 2,640 black diamonds. It weighed over 2kg!

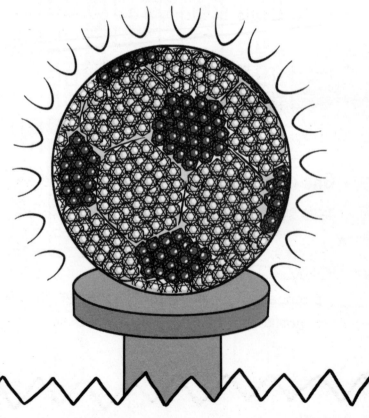

The oldest surviving football in the world is thought to date from 1540CE or earlier.

This very old football was made from a pig's bladder and covered in stitched pieces of cow leather.

It was found behind panelling in the royal bedchamber during renovations at Stirling Castle, Scotland, in the 1970s.

One of the longest goals using a header was scored 57.8m away from the goal!

Ryujiro Ueda from Japanese team Fagiano Okuyama scored from his team's half of the pitch, and the ball sailed straight over the goalkeeper from the opposing team.

There was a local football team in South Africa made up of grandmothers, some of whom were in their 80s!

It was formed in 2005 with the aim of using football to improve health. The team were called Vakhegula Vakhegula – meaning 'Grannies, Grannies' in the local Xitsonga language.

Cristiano Ronaldo built a large, two-storey museum in his hometown dedicated to... himself!

The CR7 Museum features more than 125 medals and trophies that the player has won. A five-star luxury hotel close by – Hotel CR7 – was also built by Ronaldo.

Look out for other books in the series!